Child Care

Yeow! I'm in Charge of a Human Being!

by Mary Ellis

Perfection Learning® CA

About the Author

Mary Ellis began baby-sitting when she was 12 years old. That was a long time ago, but kids really haven't changed that much. She can still remember her first nighttime job. The young parents left her with a new baby for several hours. The baby slept most of the time. Mary sat and watched the baby sleep. She listened to the wind howl through the trees outside. When the parents finally came home, they began fighting. Mary sneaked out the door and ran one block home. She never did get paid for the job. And she never went back to that house. After that, things improved. Mary had a long career of baby-sitting that lasted through her college years. In fact, her last job in college was as a nanny to a two-year-old. Today Mary lives in Texas and works with children. Her own children are grown.

Use this book as general information or as a resource to help you deal with a child of a certain age.

Note: Throughout this book, I have used the word *parents* when talking about the adults that children live with. Remember that in this book, the parents are the adults who have the job of caring for and raising the children. They may be single parents, couples, relatives, or friends.

Table of Contents

Chapter 1

First Things First

Are you "cut out" to baby-sit?

So you're thinking that baby-sitting is a good way to earn money. Well, it can be fun too. And baby-sitting can be rewarding. You're working with children *and* making money.

But first, you must ask yourself some questions. If you can answer yes to these questions, then you will probably make a very good baby-sitter.

Do you like young children?

Young children are cute. But they can be trying too. You must be able to handle their nonsense.

Little children don't have a very good sense of humor yet. What they think is funny, you might not.

They don't have much control over their feelings. They don't always know right from wrong. And they can get hurt easily.

This is all normal. They have a lot of growing to do before they are grown-up.

 So, keeping this in mind, do you really like children?

Can you allow children to be themselves?

Young children like to do the same things many times. They might want one kind of cereal over and over again. They might want you to play the same game many times. Or they may always tell you the same corny joke.

Children need to do this. They are learning about the world. Doing things over and over again helps them. Part of growing up is knowing that you aren't the center of everything. Little kids just don't know this yet. They'll want what they want, not what you want.

So, keeping this in mind, can you allow children to be themselves?

Can you keep your temper?

Young children can be very hard to handle. They can cry for a long time. They can also get so angry that they are out of control. Older children may try to play tricks on you or ignore you.

No matter what, you must be able to keep your temper. You must know that you can never hit a child in your care.

Also, you should never talk in a mean way to children. You should never try to hurt their feelings. If you have a short temper, you shouldn't baby-sit.

 So, keeping this in mind, can you keep your temper?

Are you able to be in control?

Sometimes children won't do what you ask. They may not go to bed or stay in the yard. They may ignore you if you tell them not to do something.

Rules are for children's health and safety. When you're in charge, you must be firm about the rules.

Sometimes there won't be a rule. Then you must make up the rule. You know what's right and what's safe.

 So, keeping this in mind, can you take control?

Can you keep your cool?

You should keep your cool when baby-sitting. Some things make you feel like losing your cool. Things like dirty diapers or babies who won't stop crying may frustrate you. Also children and pets making messes or someone getting cut or hurt may upset you. If you lose your cool, the children might become scared.

 So, if something bad happens, can you keep your cool?

If you answered yes to the questions above, read on. If you answered no to any of the questions, read on anyway. Maybe you just need more time to grow up. Next year, you may make the best baby-sitter ever.

Before You Baby-Sit

How many children can you handle?

The parents of two small children call. They ask you to baby-sit for them. At the last minute, the parents call back. They ask you to baby-sit more young children. What do you do?

To see if you can handle this many young children, ask yourself these questions.

- Have I baby-sat young children before?
- Do I know all the children well?
- Have I baby-sat in this house before?
- Will my family be home if I need help?

If you answer no to any of these questions, then you shouldn't baby-sit these small children. You may want to ask a friend to come and help you. You can work together. You can also share the money you earn.

How late and how much can you baby-sit?

You should check with your parents before taking a baby-sitting job. Your family may have plans. You may have homework to get done. The job may end at a late hour. Your parents will help you decide if you can baby-sit.

You should ask your parents *how much* you should baby-sit. They will help make sure you have time for homework.

You shouldn't do homework while watching the children. You are there to baby-sit.

How much should you charge?

Before you take a baby-sitting job, you should talk with the parents. Ask them how much they will pay you.

They will probably want to know what you charge. To find out what to charge, ask your friends who baby-sit what they charge.

You can charge by the hour, by the number of children, or by the job. Your parents can also help you decide what to charge.

Sometimes parents will pay extra for baby-sitting late. You might also make extra money by doing things around the house.

What are the house rules?

Before the parents leave you in charge, ask what rules the children should follow. Here are some things you need to know.

- Where are the important phone numbers?
- Can the children have friends over or talk on the phone?
- When will the children go to bed?
- What do they need to do at bedtime?
- Can the children have snacks? If so, what kind of snack is okay?
- Can the children play outside?
- Is there a family pet to take care of?

Sometimes the children can help you with the rules. Sometimes they may tell you something is a rule, but they may be making it up.

When the parents return, you can ask them about the rule. Then you'll know the next time you baby-sit.

Baby-sitting for a family gets easier the more you are there. You get to know the rules better. And you get to know the children better.

Other things to know

Once you have a baby-sitting job, you must show up. If you can't be there, call the parents right away. You should give them time to find another baby-sitter. If you do this a lot, they may quit calling you to baby-sit. Make sure you back out only when it's necessary.

Find out who will be picking you up and taking you home. Sometimes your parents may need to give you rides.

Don't ride with parents who have been drinking. Call your parents and make plans with them. Sometimes your parents aren't home. Then call your grandparents or someone else you know. Don't ride with someone who has been drinking. Even if it means they won't call you again.

When you leave, the house should be clean. If you make a mess, clean it up. The children can help clean up too.

Some people want you to do housework. They may want you to wash dishes or fold clothes. Ask parents how they want the jobs done. Also ask if they'll pay you extra.

When working for a new family, ask to come early. Tell the parents you'll come free of charge. This will help you get to know the children and the house rules. The parents can answer any questions you have.

Coming early will also help the parents and children get to know you. The parents will feel better about leaving their children with you. And you will feel better about your job.

Chapter 3

Safety First

Chapter 3 helps you know what to do in case of trouble.

For baby-sitting, you should know first-aid. Call the American Red Cross. They have first-aid training for children. Also check with your school or library.

Don't forget 911. Sometimes, bad things happen while you're baby-sitting.

What if you need help?

Sometimes, small things happen that you can't handle by yourself. You may not need to call the parents, but you still need help. There may be a stopped-up sink, a runaway pet, or a skinned knee.

Always ask the parents to leave the number of a nearby adult to call for help. You can also call your own parents. Knowing that there's someone to call will make you feel better about being in charge.

Sometimes, you may need to call the parents for help. They will want to know if their child is hurt badly or sick. They will also want to know if you are unable to handle their child.

Always ask the parents you are baby-sitting for to leave a number where they'll be. They may be able to help you over the phone. Or they may need to come home.

What if you get scared?

Sometimes, you hear noises. Houses make noises most of the time. You just don't always hear them.

Don't lose your cool if you hear noises. See if you can tell what the noise is. It may be a window rattling. It may be the heat coming on. When you know what the noise is, you'll feel better.

You can hear noises outside the house too. Again, listen and see if you can tell what the noise is. If you think someone is trying to get in, call 911. Tell them what you hear. They will help you know what to do.

You may find that the noise wasn't someone trying to get in. Don't feel bad about calling 911. It's always better to be safe than sorry.

Important things to know

Try to learn as much about the children as you can. Make your own form like the one shown on the next page to write this information down. Give the form to the parents a few days before you baby-sit. They can fill it out for you.

Use the back of your form to jot down other important things you learn as you baby-sit. This may be helpful for you the next time.

Make many copies of your form. Keep them in a folder. Take the folder with you when you baby-sit. The form will help you keep track of everything, and the parents will know you are trying to be a good baby-sitter.

Here are some things you will want to know before you baby-sit.

Family name _____

Address _____

Phone number _____

Phone number where parents will be _____

Emergency phone numbers _____
_____
_____

Children's names and ages _____
_____
_____
_____

Medical and health information _____
_____
_____
_____

Bedtime _____

Snacks _____

Special rules _____
_____
_____

Notes and special information _____
_____
_____

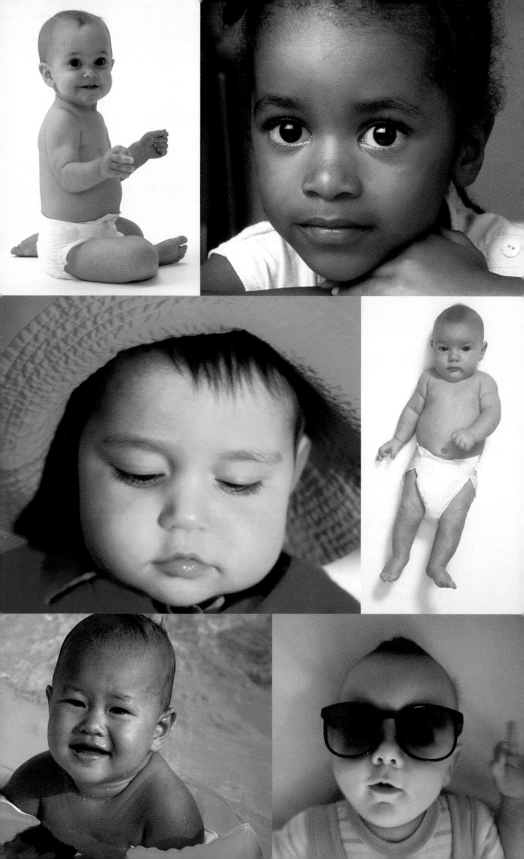

Chapter 4

Babies
(newborn–18 months)

Babies are small and helpless. They need a lot of attention. It can be hard to know why a baby is crying. You should check for these things.

- Is she hungry?
- Is she upset?
- Is she tired?
- Does she need a diaper change?

Is the baby hungry?

The parents should tell you how to feed the baby. You need to know when and what to feed him and how to feed him.

You should hold a tiny baby while you feed him. You can also set him in an infant seat. Hold the bottle up. Make sure the baby isn't getting air. This can make him feel bad.

You may feed the baby cereal or baby food with a spoon. Use a small spoon. Get just a little bit of food in each bite.

Make sure the food or milk is about the same temperature as the baby. You may need to warm it up. Ask the parents to show you how to do this.

Make sure the food or the bottle isn't too hot. The parents should show you how to test them.

Here is one way to test food or milk. Put a little on the inside of your arm. If it feels hot, let it cool before giving it to the baby.

You should burp babies after they have eaten. There are different ways you can burp a baby.

- Put him up against your chest. Rest his head against you. Gently rub or pat his back.
- Sit the baby up on your lap. Cup his chin in your hand. Then, gently rub or pat his back.

Sometimes babies burp right away. Other times, it may take a while. Don't get rough or in a hurry.

Once the baby has burped, he may want to eat more. You can feed him until he doesn't want to eat anymore. Then you may need to burp him again.

Is the baby upset?

Sometimes babies cry because they hurt. Sometimes their tummies hurt. It may take a while before the baby feels better. Here are some things you can try to help the baby feel better.

20

- Rub her back.
- Lay her against your chest and hold her against you.
- Hold her on your lap in a sitting position.
- Hold her against your chest while you walk around.
- Sit or stand, and rock her.
- Talk or sing to her.

Sometimes none of these things helps a baby feel better. Then you must stay calm. Remember that every baby is different. What works for one baby may not work for another. Also, what works one time may not work the next time. Keep your cool if she won't stop crying.

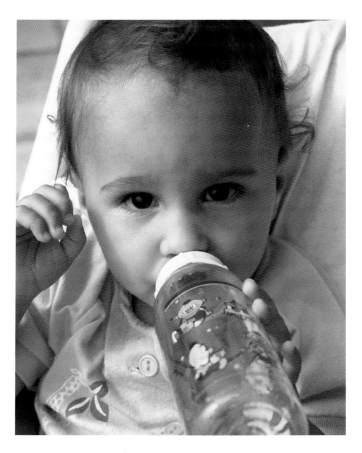

If you have tried everything and are losing your cool, put the baby in her bed. Step away from the bed for a few minutes. Get better control of yourself. Then try to help the baby again.

Is the baby tired?

Some babies will go right to sleep when they've been fed and changed. You lay them down in their beds. They smile sweetly at you. They close their eyes and go to sleep. You are a lucky baby-sitter if this happens.

Most other babies want more attention at bedtime. Make sure your attention is quiet and peaceful. This helps the baby stay calm so he can fall asleep.

Little babies like to hear a story before bed. They like to hear your voice. Babies like to be rocked. Sing a quiet song as you rock the baby.

The next trick is putting him to bed. Remember to move slowly and gently. Good luck!

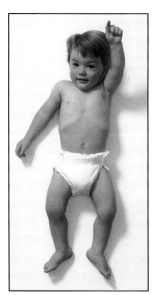

Does the baby need a diaper change?

Changing a diaper is hard. It's something you have to practice before you're good at it. Not many people like doing it.

It's hard to tell someone how to change a diaper. You should learn by watching. Ask the parents to show you how. Then try it yourself. Always wash your hands with soap after changing a diaper.

Check the diaper often. Babies don't like to wear dirty diapers. Dirty diapers can cause a rash that hurts.

You should ask before putting anything on the baby's bottom. Parents should also tell you where you should put dirty diapers.

Most parents won't want you to bathe a baby. If you need to, you can gently rub him with a warm, wet cloth.

Keeping a baby happy

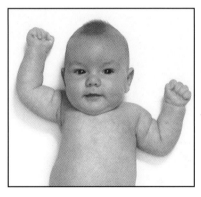

Babies love attention. They are learning a great deal at this age. They love to watch what's going on around them.

Set the baby where she can see you. She will enjoy following you with her eyes. If you're watching another child, the baby may be happy just looking at the two of you.

Babies like it when you talk to them. Look the baby in the eyes and talk away. If you smile, she might smile back. She may even start "talking" to you.

If you are caring for an older baby that moves around, be sure to keep her safe. Play with the baby with her own toys. Don't let her play with small things. Babies will put small things in their mouths. They can choke on small things.

Never swing a baby around or play rough. Playing with babies in this way is not safe.

Play with their toys instead. Talk and sing to the baby. Play games like Pat-a-Cake and Peek-a-Boo. These games help babies grow up.

Chapter 5

Toddlers
(18 months–3 years)

A toddler is still a baby in many ways. He may still wear diapers and talk baby talk.

But toddlers get around more because they are walking. Most toddlers also run and climb. They do things that can be unsafe.

Toddlers don't think about being safe. You should think about this for them.

Almost everything you learned about babies goes for toddlers. Except the burping part. (Toddlers can burp on their own. They don't always say "excuse me.")

Baby-sitting toddlers is a lot of work. They move around fast and need your attention. You should probably baby-sit only one toddler at a time.

Feeding a toddler

Some toddlers still drink from a bottle. They can do this by themselves. But most toddlers drink from a cup.

Toddlers love to feed themselves. They may think it's funny to put food where it doesn't belong. They may put the food in their hair, ears, or nose. They may try to put the food in your hair too. Toddlers also like to throw food.

These things are messy and unsafe. You have to be firm and tell them "no." You can say no without being mean.

Ask the parents what the toddler can eat. It is normal if a toddler doesn't want to eat. Don't force him. Just let him play. He'll let you know when he's hungry.

Playing with a toddler

Toddlers love to play with simple puzzles, blocks, and games. They also like playing with stacking rings and large balls. Pans and boxes are fun too.

 **26**

Toddlers love to explore. Take them for a walk inside the house. Let them show you things. Look out windows or look in mirrors.

If it's okay to go outside, take a walk around the house. Try to find bugs to watch. Listen for special noises.

Toddlers are very busy learning to talk. If you talk a lot to them, they will probably talk back to you. You may not understand what they're saying. If you don't understand, just nod your head and keep talking. Talking to toddlers helps them learn to talk.

If the toddler gets upset, try to change the subject or start singing a song. You can also put on some music and get her to dance with you. You can talk again later, when she is not upset.

Toddlers like to know how things work. They like to put things away and then get them out again. This can become a fun game. You'll get tired of it before the toddler will.

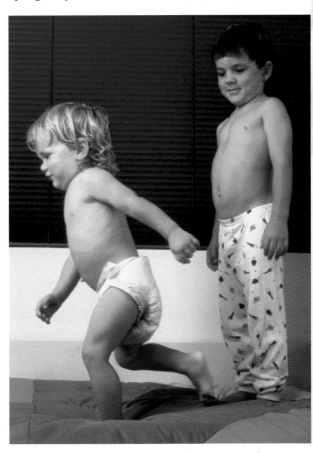

Toddlers like to move around a lot. They like to dance, roll around, cuddle, and jump on the floor.

Some things are too wild to do indoors. Outdoor things that can be fun for toddlers are running, jumping around, and riding a tricycle. They may like pushing a stroller or spinning around.

A toddler's temper

Toddlers are just finding out about their world. They are beginning to feel some power. They want to do things by themselves. But they aren't big enough to do many things on their own.

Adults might not let them try to do things. This can make toddlers mad. When toddlers get mad, they might cry. They might feel better with a hug from you. It might also help if you can find something they can do.

Some toddlers have temper tantrums when they get mad. It's hard to handle a toddler having a temper tantrum. He may scream, cry, bite, kick, or throw things. He may do all of those things.

Sometimes temper tantrums can stop quickly. If the toddler doesn't stop, here are some things to try.

- Stay in the same room with him to make sure he is safe. But leave him alone.

- Do something that you know the toddler will want to do.
- Take the toddler to another room or outdoors if possible.

After a while, the temper tantrum will stop. The toddler will become interested in something else.

When the temper tantrum is over, act like nothing happened. Chances are the toddler will do the same.

How to get a toddler to mind you

This is a mystery. Sometimes you can get a toddler to do something by asking her. At other times, nothing works.

Offer a reward to a toddler who doesn't want to mind. Tell her she can be the fairy princess first, choose the snack, or pick a story to read. If the reward sounds good to the toddler, she may mind you.

Show the toddler what you want her to do. If it's time to pick up toys, you begin. Put a toy away. Then tell her that you get the prize. Most toddlers want what you have. So she may pick up a toy too.

Make cleanup time into a game. You can race to see who can finish first. You can see who can pick up the most toys. You might set a timer and see if you can get done before it buzzes. Toddlers love to play games!

Sometimes a toddler still won't mind you. In this case, stay calm. Yelling and being mean won't make the toddler mind. Find something else to do for a while.

How to get a toddler to go to bed

Most toddlers are very busy when they're awake. So they're ready for bed at night.

If a toddler won't go to bed, don't get mad. He may just need more time to settle down. Try reading a book aloud while he sits on your lap. Singing a quiet song will also help make him tired.

When he begins to get tired, move him to the bed. You can still read the story or sing. Yawn a few times and rub your eyes. All of this will help him get sleepy.

The only trouble is, you may get sleepy too!

Chapter 6

Preschoolers (3–5 years)

Preschoolers are fun to baby-sit. They can talk to you. They can do many things for themselves.

Preschoolers are easier to handle than toddlers. But some preschoolers still have temper tantrums. Handle them just as you would with a toddler. Chances are, he'll feel silly and stop. He'll see that having a temper tantrum won't help him.

Playing with a preschooler

Most preschoolers like to move around. They like to play games. They have a lot of energy. They learn by doing things.

Preschoolers love puzzles and simple board games. They like to build things with blocks. They like to crawl inside and under things.

Build a tent by throwing a blanket over a table or between chairs. Take an old toy or game of your own to their house. Kids love to play with other people's toys. It's like having a new toy for a few hours.

How to get a preschooler to mind you

Preschoolers will mind better than toddlers. They like to please other people. But some preschoolers won't mind. They will try to explain why they shouldn't have to do something. Just tell them again nicely. Try not to argue.

If the preschooler won't mind, try offering her a reward. Preschoolers like special things too.

Sometimes a preschooler will try to hide from you. He will want you to look for him. This may not be safe. Try to find something else to play.

Images © 1996 PhotoDisc, Inc.

35

How to get a preschooler to go to bed

Most preschoolers will mind about going to bed. They want to please you.

Sometimes you will baby-sit a preschooler who won't go to sleep. All you can do is keep smiling and tucking in. Keep saying that it's bedtime. Don't get upset.

Most preschoolers like being read to. Some have a story they like to hear over and over. Many will be able to "read" you the story. They know it by heart because they've heard it so many times.

Let your preschooler choose the bedtime story. She may want you to read it more than once. You are helping her learn to read by reading to her. Don't try to teach her to read each word. Just read. She's learning by watching you.

36

If you have a favorite book at home, take it along with you. Chances are, the preschooler will enjoy it too.

Some preschoolers are afraid of the dark. Some have nightmares. If the child asks you to leave a light on, go ahead. Night-lights, hall lights, and closet lights work best. This will help her feel better.

If you read a book before bedtime, don't make it a scary one! The preschooler will be too afraid to be left alone. You might also scare yourself!

Images © 1996 PhotoDisc, Inc.

Chapter 7

School-Age Kids
(6 years and up)

By the time children are in school, they can talk well. They'll let you know what they need and how they feel. They may also tell you what you're doing wrong.

Every child is different. Some are shy. Some are outgoing. Some want to please you. Some don't. Some are bossy. Some are tricky. You will need to handle them in different ways. Always use common sense and treat children kindly.

With school-age children, the baby-sitting job may seem easy. You may think that you don't have to pay as much attention to children this age.

Just remember that baby-sitting is a job. Your job is to care for the children. You still need to play with school-age children. You need to give them your attention.

You may not know it, but you are a role model for school-age children. They may want to be just like you. Always be a good role model.

Playing with school-age children

Some children may find one quiet thing to do for a long time. Or they may move from one thing to another. Whatever they are doing, you must keep track of them.

Most school-age kids love to have an older child to play with. This is how they learn.

Keep a list of games. You can play Slap Jack or Crazy Eights with a deck of cards. With some string, you can play Cat's Cradle. You can play Connect-the-Dots or Hangman with pencil and paper.

Chapter 9 tells you how to play these games and others.

You can also help children with their homework or draw with them. You can walk around the block or just sit and talk. You can bake cookies or play computer games.

Images © 1996 PhotoDisc, Inc.

How to get school-age children to mind you

Sometimes the children may be as big as you are. But you are still in charge. You know the rules. You must make sure the children follow them.

Some school-age children want to be in charge themselves. Let them know that their parents are paying you to be in charge. Let them know in a firm but nice way that they have to follow the rules.

Most school-age children listen to older children. They will like it when you give them your attention.

Some families may not have a special bedtime. As it begins to get late, find quiet things for the kids to do.

If it's okay to have a snack, have something that won't keep them awake. Have milk and cookies, fruit, or crackers.

Children this age may still like it when you read to them. They may even want to read a book to you.

Handling school-age children can be tricky. If you let them know you're in charge and treat them with respect, they will mind you. They'll want you to come back the next time.

Baby-sitting older children

Sometimes you may baby-sit children almost your age! They may just need your help watching younger children.

Also, even older children can get scared when they're alone. Your job might be to keep them company.

Sometimes older children don't like having a baby-sitter. Let them know that you are there to be a friend and to help them.

Chapter 8

Other Stuff

This chapter will help you handle special times.

Children who fight

When you are baby-sitting more than one child, they may fight. Children fight for many reasons. If you have brothers or sisters, you may have done the same thing.

Sometimes children fight by yelling at each other. But sometimes they hit each other.

Always try to stop a fight before it gets out of hand. Tell the children to go to different rooms. Give them time to cool off.

When everyone has settled down, get together to talk about the problem. See if you can find and fix the problem together.

If children won't listen to you, stay calm. Call the parents at the phone number they left. Tell them what is

happening. Maybe they can help you over the phone. Or they may need to come home and take care of the problem.

Don't feel bad about calling the parents if you have tried everything to keep control.

Children who are scared

Small children can get scared when their parents leave them. They may get upset and cry. Hold their hands and let them know that you will take care of them. Try to get them interested in a toy or game. After a while, they won't be upset anymore.

Children sometimes get scared after going to bed. Sit with them and talk softly. Pat or rub their backs. Read a short story to them. This will help settle them down so they can go back to sleep. It is not a good idea to let them get up.

Children who are handicapped

Someday, you might baby-sit a child who's handicapped. The parents will help you know how to care for their child.

Don't be afraid to ask questions before the parents leave. Also, don't be afraid to ask the child questions.

There's an old saying that goes like this: "Knowledge is power." The more questions you ask, the more you know. The more you know, the better you'll feel about baby-sitting a handicapped child.

Children who are just plain rotten

You might baby-sit a child who won't do anything you say. She may act nasty and treat you mean.

If you have tried to handle the problem, call the parents or another adult. Don't be afraid to ask for help.

Kids you want to baby-sit again and again

Baby-sitting is good for you and the families you work for. The children get to learn from you. They get to make a "big-kid" friend. They have another good role model. And the parents get a break.

You get to earn your own money. You're also learning when you baby-sit. You're learning how to get along with people of all ages. You're learning how to be a parent someday.

Fun and Games

Kids love to learn new games. This chapter tells you how to play many games. You may have played these games when you were younger. You don't need many things to play them.

Copy these games into your baby-sitting notebook. Then you'll always have good ideas about what to play.

Card games

Go Fish (age 4 and up)

Needed: one deck of playing cards
Number of players: 2
The object of the game is to get the most pairs of cards. (A pair of cards is two cards with the same number on them.)

- Shuffle and deal seven cards to each player.
- Put the rest of the cards face down in a pile. This is the pickup pile.
- The dealer begins play by asking for a card.
- If the other player has the card, she has to give it to him.

- He continues asking until the other player doesn't have the card and says "go fish." This means the dealer draws a card from the pickup pile.
- Now it's the other player's turn to ask for a card.
- As players make pairs, they should lay them face down on the table.
- Play continues until one player lays down all of her cards in pairs. She is the winner.

Concentration (age 4 and up)

Needed: one deck of playing cards
Number of players: 2
The object of the game is to find the most pairs of cards.

- Shuffle and spread out all cards face down on a table.
- Each player takes turns turning two cards face up.
- If the cards match, that player keeps the pair and takes another turn.
- If the cards don't match, the player turns them face down again and the other person takes a turn.
- When all cards have been paired, the game is over. The player with the most pairs is the winner.

Slapjack (age 4 and up)

Needed: one deck of playing cards
Number of players: 2 to 6
The object of the game is to win all the cards in the deck.

- Shuffle and deal all cards face down to players.

- The dealer takes his top card and turns it up in the middle of the table.
- If it's a Jack, all players try to slap their hand on it first. The person who slaps the Jack first takes it and all cards underneath.
- If it isn't a Jack, the next person takes a turn.
- If a person slaps a card that isn't a Jack, he puts all of his cards in the pile in the center of the table. He can continue to play by trying to slap the Jack and get some cards again.
- When one person has all the cards, the game is over and that person is the winner.

Crazy Eights (age 4 and up)

Needed: one deck of playing cards
Number of players: 2 to 4
The object of the game is to get rid of all your cards.

- Shuffle and deal 7 cards to each player.
- Stack the rest of the cards on the table. This is the pickup pile. Turn the top card face up.
- Beginning with the dealer, each player tries to match the card next to the pickup pile. He can match it by playing a card with the same number or the same suit. If he is unable to match the card, he may play an 8. Then he can say what number or suit the next player has to match.
- If a player is unable to match, he must take cards from the pickup pile until he can match.
- The first player to get rid of all of her cards is the winner.

Games with strings

Cat's Cradle (age 7 and up)

Needed: a long string or yarn, tied in a loop

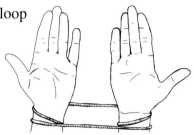

- Loop the string around both wrists, and then wrap the string around wrists one time.

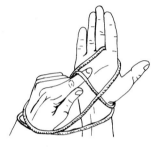

- Pick up string from right wrist with left pointer finger. Let string loop behind your finger.

- Pick up string from left wrist with right pointer finger. Let string loop behind your finger.

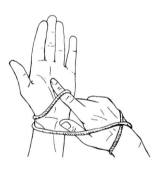

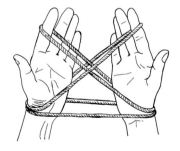

- Pull the string tight. You have made the Cat's Cradle.

You can work with a partner and make more string pictures. Use the book *Cat's Cradle and Other String Figures* by Bab Westerveld (Penguin, 1979) for lots of ideas.

Games with paper and pencil

Connect-the-Dots (age 5 and up)

Needed: Paper and pencils
Number of players: any number can play this game
The object is to complete as many squares as you can.

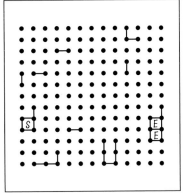

- Evenly space dots in rows and columns on a sheet of paper.
- Players take turns drawing lines across or down to connect 2 dots.
- Each time a player completes a box, she writes her initials inside the box.
- Play continues until all squares are made. The player with her initials in the most squares is the winner.

Hangman (age 7 and up)

Needed: Paper and pencils
Number of players: 2 to 4
The winner is the first person to guess what the word is.

- One player thinks of a word and makes as many dashes on a sheet of paper as there are letters in the word. He also makes a gallows for the hangman. (see picture)

- The other player begins guessing letters.
- If the letter is in the word, it is written in the correct dash.
- If the letter is not in the word, a body part is drawn on the gallows.
- A player wins by guessing the word before the entire hangman is drawn.

Games with your hands

Paper-Scissors-Rock (age 4 and up)

Number of players: 2
The object is to try to get the most points.

- Players count to three and position their hands in one of the following signs.
  - Hand in a fist = rock
  - Hand laid open = paper
  - Two fingers in a V-shape = scissors

- Rock wins over scissors, paper wins over rock, and scissors wins over paper.

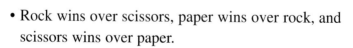

- Each winner gets a point. Play until you reach 10 or more points.

Double Thumb Wrestling (age 4 and up)

Number of players: 2 or any even number
The object is to try to pin down another person's thumb with your thumb.

- Two players stand across from each other. Four or more players form a circle.
- Grab hands by hooking fingers together and pointing thumbs up.
- At the count of 3, each player tries to pin the other's thumb down using his own thumb.
- The winner is the person who pins the other player's thumb down first.

Bedtime Stories

 Bedtime Mouse by Sandol Stoddard. At bedtime, a child finds all sorts of wonderful things, not only around the house, but also in his very own head. Houghton, 1993.

 Can't You Sleep, Little Bear? by Martin Waddell. Little Bear is afraid of "the darkness all around" him until Big Bear helps him face his fear and realize the beauty of the night. Candlewick, 1994.

📖 *Dark Night, Sleepy Night* by Harriet Ziefert. Illustrations and a simple text show animals asleep in their natural surroundings. Puffin, 1993.

📖 *The Goodnight Circle* by Carolyn Lesser. As the turtle pulls in his head and the bullfrog settles into his squishy mud bed, the night animals wake up. The peepers, owls, beavers, and water snakes learn, eat, play, and then sleep, completing the cycle of the Goodnight Circle. Harcourt, 1991.

📖 *Goodnight Moon* by Margaret Wise Brown. A little rabbit says goodnight to each thing in his room. Scholastic, 1993.

📖 *Grandfather Twilight* by Barbara Helen Berger. This myth describes the beauty and wonder of the coming of twilight and the rising of the moon. Putnam, 1992.

📖 *The Moonglow Roll-a-Rama* by Dav Pilkey. This story tells what animals really do when the rest of the world is asleep. Orchard, 1995.

📖 *Once: A Lullaby* by B. P. Nichol. Young animals and children are shown in the moments just before they fall asleep. Morrow, 1992.

📖 *Sleep Song* by Karen Ray. Rhymes copy the sounds a child hears while preparing for bedtime. Orchard, 1995.

📖 *Sleep Tight, Pete* by Ellen Schecter. Pete loves bedtime stories—especially when they are all about him! Bantam, 1995.

Sleepy Dog by Harriet Ziefert. A cuddly little dog and his pet cat share goodnight kisses and playful dreams in this magical bedtime story. Random, 1984.

Ten, Nine, Eight by Molly Bang. Numbers from 10 to 1 are part of this lullaby about the room of a little girl going to bed. Scholastic, 1993.

When Sheep Cannot Sleep: The Counting Book by Satoshi Kitamura. In this counting book, a sheep finds things to count to order to go to sleep. Farrar, 1988.

Where Does the Brown Bear Go? by Nicki Weiss. Follow the animals as they head to the safety of a child's bed for the night. Puffin, 1990.

Wynken, Blynken, and Nod by Eugene Field. This is the tale of a magical moonlight sail in a wooden shoe. This is one of the most beloved bedtime poems of childhood in full-color paintings. Scholastic, 1993.